EVALUATING THE GENDER EQUALITY AND SOCIAL INCLUSION IMPACTS OF ADB-FINANCED PROJECTS IN SOUTH ASIA

A GUIDANCE NOTE

DECEMBER 2023

ASIAN DEVELOPMENT BANK

Note:
In this publication, "$" refers to United States dollars.

On the cover: Beneficiaries from the Urban Governance and Infrastructure Improvement Project in Bangladesh (photo by Carola Molitor).

Cover design by Josef Ilumin.

Contents

APPENDIXES

Tables, Figure, and Box

TABLES

FIGURE

BOX

Abbreviations

ADB	Asian Development Bank
CPS	country partnership strategy
DFID	Department for International Development of the United Kingdom
DMC	developing member country
DMF	design and monitoring framework
GAP	gender action plan
GESI	gender equality and social inclusion
OP	operational priority
OP1	operational priority 1
OP2	operational priority 2
PCR	project completion report
RFI	results framework indicator
SARD	South Asia Department
SOGIESC	sexual orientation, gender identity and expression, and sex characteristics

CHAPTER 1
Introduction

A. General Contents and Purpose of this Guidance Note

1.   This guidance note presents an overview of approaches for evaluating the gender equality and social inclusion (GESI) impacts of projects financed by the Asian Development Bank (ADB) in South Asia. It aims to provide ADB South Asia Department (SARD) GESI team, project teams, and partner project executing and implementing agencies with key points to consider in designing the terms of reference for project impact evaluation or assessment, and in supervising the impact evaluation or assessment process and reporting. The guidance note also provides resources or references that the SARD GESI team, project team, or executing and/or implementing agency may use if they opt to do the evaluation or assessment themselves.[1]

2.   In this guidance note, GESI impact evaluation refers to the measurement and/or description of the intended and unintended GESI results of SARD's programs and projects. A specific project's GESI-related intended results are based on the GESI performance indicators and targets in the project's design and monitoring framework (DMF) and GESI action plan. These indicators and targets are linked to ADB's GESI-related corporate results framework and tracking indicators.[2] The unintended results are unexpected or unplanned. GESI impacts can be immediate, intermediate, or long-term results of the project interventions.

B. Gender Equality and Social Inclusion Impacts: Overall Guiding Frameworks and Definitions

3.   The promotion of GESI is in line with ADB's Strategy 2030, particularly operational priority 1 (OP1): "addressing remaining poverty and reducing inequalities," and operational priority 2 (OP2): "accelerating progress in gender equality."[3] To operationalize the mandates of Strategy 2030 OP1 and OP2 in the context of South Asia, SARD has prepared a GESI framework, which presents its guiding GESI principles and definitions of relevant concepts, an overview of the GESI situation in South Asia, and SARD's seven key areas of action for GESI. This guidance note serves as a tool for the sixth key area of action: capturing GESI results by engaging in strategic and

---

[1]   This guidance note should be used as complementary to any other core guidance issued by ADB's Strategy, Policy, and Partnerships Department and its Sustainable Development and Climate Change Department, including the Gender Tip Sheets. ADB. Gender Tip Sheets.
[2]   ADB. 2019. ADB Corporate Results Framework, 2019-2024: Policy Paper. Manila; ADB. 2023. Tracking Indicator Definitions. Manila.
[3]   ADB. 2018. *Strategy 2030: Achieving a Prosperous, Inclusive, Resilient, and Sustainable Asia and the Pacific.* Manila.

innovative impact evaluations.[4] The programs' or projects' GESI impacts to be identified are essentially related to the three pillars of OP1 and the five pillars of OP2, as well as to the results of initiatives addressing the intersection of gender inequality (OP2) and other sources of exclusion and discrimination (OP1).[5]

4.   In line with its GESI framework, SARD gives special attention to (as relevant to the evaluated project) the following dimensions of exclusion and vulnerability across its six developing member countries (DMCs): (i) gender; (ii) age (older persons and disadvantaged youth); (iii) disability; (iv) social identities (e.g., caste, ethnicity, and religion); (v) diverse sexual orientation, gender identity and expression, and sex characteristics (SOGIESC); (vi) geographic location; (vii) income status; and (viii) migrant status.[6] Among excluded and vulnerable individuals and groups, more focused attention is given to those experiencing intersecting inequalities and discrimination because of their overlapping disadvantaged identities.

5.   As impact evaluation examines whether changes in project areas can be attributed to project interventions and not to other factors, it is often associated with quantitative methods capable of counterfactual analysis.[7] In counterfactual analysis, changes in project areas or outcomes of project interventions are compared with changes or outcomes that would have occurred without the project intervention. As qualitative methods are not capable of counterfactual analysis and are often associated with exploratory research or are used when prior knowledge of the project's potential outcomes is unavailable, they are sometimes regarded as merely playing a supporting role to quantitative methods. Nonetheless, since the last decades of the twentieth century, the relevance of qualitative methods has been gaining more ground, especially with the acknowledgment of three limitations of the quantitative method revolving around the inability of the quantitative method to capture (i) the subjective meanings that a respondent gives to their answers to a structured question; (ii) the political, social, and gender context (e.g., socioeconomic and political conditions, and social and gender norms) of the answers; and (iii) the way the respondent positions the evaluator or project proponents (e.g., trustworthy or not, or capable or not of helping solve their problems).[8] Addressing these limitations and recognizing the significance of qualitative methods are important for the evaluation of GESI impacts.

6.   Specifically, apart from examining if GESI-related improvements in project areas can be attributed to project interventions, GESI impact evaluation also seeks to bring to the surface the common and distinct meanings that women, men, girls, boys, and people with diverse SOGIESC, especially those belonging to excluded and vulnerable groups, in project areas give to the project interventions and GESI-related outcomes because of their socioeconomic, political, and gender contexts.[9] It also seeks to remove, as far as possible, the power imbalance between the researcher and the researched (or subject), and to enable women and excluded and vulnerable groups to become empowered by the research process through participatory impact evaluation methods.

---

[4]   Before proceeding to the next sections of this guidance note, readers are advised to read SARD's GESI framework. The definitions of related key concepts, including groups affected by inequality, exclusion, vulnerability, and intersectionality, are included in the SARD GESI framework and hence are not repeated here. ADB. 2023. *Framework for Integrating Gender Equality and Social Inclusion in South Asia Department Operations.* Manila.

[5]   The three pillars of OP1 are (i) human capital and social protection enhanced for all, (ii) quality jobs generated, and (iii) opportunities for the most vulnerable people or persons increased. The five pillars of OP2 are (i) women's economic empowerment increased, (ii) gender equality in human development enhanced, (iii) gender equality in decision-making and leadership enhanced, (iv) women's time poverty and drudgery reduced, and (v) women's resilience to external shocks strengthened.

[6]   ADB. 2023. *Framework for Integrating Gender Equality and Social Inclusion in South Asia Department Operations.* Manila.

[7]   ADB's practical guide on impact evaluation and the World Bank's handbook on impact evaluation focus on the quantitative methods. H. White and D. A. Raitzer. 2017. *Impact Evaluation of Development Interventions: A Practical Guide.* Manila: ADB; and S. R. Khandker, G. B. Koolwal, and H. A. Samad. 2010. *Handbook on Impact Evaluation: Quantitative Methods and Practices.* Washington, DC: World Bank.

[8]   U. Flick. 2009. *An Introduction to Qualitative Research.* Fourth Edition. London: SAGE Publications.

[9]   Similar principles (but focused solely on women) are found here: Policy, Action, Research List. Resources. Introduction to Feminist Research. Written by Jennifer Brayton, Michele Olivier, and Wendy Robbins.

7.   SARD's GESI impact evaluation is guided by these principles and the three pillars of the leave-no-one-behind framework of the former Department for International Development of the United Kingdom, now the Foreign, Commonwealth and Development Office. These pillars are (i) understand for action, (ii) empower for change, and (iii) include for opportunity. Appendix 1 provides examples of GESI impact evaluation questions based on these three pillars arranged according to the Strategy 2030 OP 1 and OP 2 pillars. In general, these questions cover the assessment of the effectiveness of actions to address the three pillars.[10]

(i)   **Understand for action.** Identify the barriers to GESI and analyze the capacities of women and excluded and vulnerable groups to claim their rights and promote GESI based on disaggregated data and evidence.

(ii)   **Empower for change.** Promote the livelihood, voice, and social empowerment of women and excluded and vulnerable groups.

(iii)   **Include for opportunity.** Ensure the GESI responsiveness of the social, political, and physical environment, including infrastructures, technologies, resources, and services.

C.   Key Definitions

8.   The following are the definitions of key approaches, which are further elaborated in Part IV of this guidance note:

(i)   **Impact evaluation versus impact assessment.** Both terms refer to measuring or describing the impacts of an intervention. The difference is in the scope and manner of data collection and analysis for measuring the impacts. The conventional method for impact evaluation is a randomized control trial, which statistically analyzes the significance of the differences between a reference or treatment group (composed of those affected by the project intervention) and a comparison or control group (composed of those who did not take part in the project) before and after the project intervention. However, a randomized control trial cannot be used when project baseline data (collected before the intervention or project implementation) are unavailable, in which case an impact assessment is done, where appropriate statistical methods that do not require baseline data, such as quasi-experimental design, are used.[11]

(ii)   **Nimble evaluations.** This is a type of evaluation that (i) is short term (3 to 6 months), (ii) uses available secondary data or an administrative dataset or collects few primary data, and (iii) is less expensive than a long-term (more than 6 months) evaluation that collects and analyzes large primary data (box).

(iii)   **Quantitative, qualitative, and mixed methods in evaluation research.** These are established research methods used in impact evaluations and assessments. As the terms connote, the quantitative method collects quantitative data and uses statistical methods to analyze project impacts, the qualitative method collects qualitative data and uses qualitative methods to analyze the project's benefits to targeted beneficiaries, and the mixed method is a combination of the quantitative and qualitative methods.

---

[10]   For further explanations on SARD's adaptation of the three pillars of the leave no one behind framework, see SARD's GESI framework (footnote 6); ADB. 2023. *Gender Equality and Social Inclusion Analysis to Inform ADB's Country Partnership Strategies and Project Designs in South Asia: A Guidance Note.* Manila; and ADB. Forthcoming. *Gender Equality and Social Inclusion in South Asia: An Assessment for Action.* Manila.

[11]   This differentiation of impact evaluation and assessment is for the purpose of this guidance note and may not be generally used.

Box: Nimble and Long-Term Evaluations

A nimble evaluation or assessment is a short-term (about 6 months or less) and, therefore, less expensive study. This is feasible when the following apply:
- Administrative data (collected and stored during operations) of the government or other organizations on GESI indicators are available and accessible; use of these data will lessen the time for primary data collection.
- The study has few GESI variables or performance indicators (as stated in the project's design and monitoring framework and GESI action plan); therefore, the questionnaire is short and can be administered quickly.
- The GESI impact evaluation or attribution (statistical) analysis will not require a large number of samples (respondents and/or observations), and the targeted respondents can easily be reached in terms of location and/or available technology (phone or internet).

If all the above conditions are not present, then long-term impact evaluation (i.e., involving more variables, a large number of samples, and, therefore, more expensive) may be needed. However, as feasible, nimble evaluation is recommended because the reporting time will not be far from the data collection, which means the analysis is based on more recent or real-time data. Therefore, at less cost and using real-time data, a nimble evaluation could be more cost-effective and useful.

GESI = gender equality and social inclusion.

Source: World Bank, Strategic Impact Evaluation Fund. 2021. Learning from nimble evaluations. Video recording from the Learning from nimble evaluations seminar. 11 February.

CHAPTER 2

ADB'S Frameworks for Defining and Evaluating the Gender Equality and Social Inclusion Results of Operations

9.   This section presents an overview of ADB's current framework and mechanisms for defining the targeted GESI impacts of its supported programs and projects and reporting the GESI results of its operations.

A.   ADB's Frameworks for Defining Gender Equality and Social Inclusion Impacts

10.   The targeted GESI impacts of ADB operations are defined in the following documents:

(i)   **Strategy 2030.** This contains ADB's overall development vision and operational priorities (OPs). Under Strategy 2030, ADB aims to "sustain its efforts to eradicate extreme poverty and expand its vision to achieve a prosperous, inclusive, resilient, and sustainable Asia and the Pacific."[12] Strategy 2030 has seven OPs aligned with the United Nations' Sustainable Development Goals. OP1 and OP2 are directly related to GESI, while the other five OPs also mention GESI as an overarching objective (footnote 3). The operational and implementation approaches and results (including indicators) for all seven OPs, including OP1 and OP2, are fleshed out in their respective operational plans.[13]

(ii)   **Corporate Results Framework, 2019–2024.** This provides the results framework indicators (RFIs) and tracking indicators of Strategy 2030's seven OPs.[14] It contains 60 RFIs arranged in a four-level structure.[15] Level 1, which tracks development progress in Asia and the Pacific, has 10 RFIs to monitor the region's development progress resulting from collective efforts (Appendix 2). Of these 10 RFIs, 7 are directly relevant to GESI. Level 2 RFIs are on the results from completed operations, which measure the progress against each OP. OP1 has three RFIs, and OP2 has six RFIs, one of which is the percentage of completed operations delivering intended gender equality results. Of the 14 RFIs of the other 5 OPs, 9 are directly relevant to GESI. Level 3 underscores the gender commitments of ADB's operational management: (a) committed operations classified gender equity theme or effective gender mainstreaming (%) (sovereign

---

12   Footnote 3, p. v.
13   ADB. 2019. *Strategy 2030 Operational Plan for Priority 1: Addressing Remaining Poverty and Reducing Inequalities, 2019–2024*. Manila; and ADB. 2019. *Strategy 2030 Operational Plan for Priority 2: Accelerating Progress in Gender Equality, 2019–2024*. Manila.
14   ADB. 2019. *ADB Corporate Results Framework, 2019–2024*. Manila.
15   Section I, consisting of level 1, tracks the collective regional development progress made by ADB's DMCs throughout Asia and the Pacific. Section II, consisting of levels 2, 3, and 4, measures ADB's performance in executing Strategy 2030. Level 2 focuses on the results of ADB operations that support the seven OPs. Level 3 tracks ADB's performance in selecting, designing, financing, and implementing operations. Level 4 examines ADB's performance in managing the internal resources and processes that support its operations ADB. ADB Results Framework.

and nonsovereign), and (b) committed operations classified gender equity theme, effective gender mainstreaming, or some gender elements (%) (sovereign and nonsovereign).[16]

(iii) **Country partnership strategy.** This is ADB's primary platform for designing operations to deliver development results in each DMC. ADB develops a country partnership strategy (CPS) for each of its DMCs in collaboration with the government and in consultation with other stakeholders, such as civil society organizations.[17] In developing the CPS, the regional departments, among others, prepare or update the country gender (or GESI) assessment, which helps ADB in formulating its gender or GESI strategy in the country.[18] The process involves analyzing available recent data disaggregated by sex or gender[19] and other social categories on social and economic indicators, including gender and social inequalities in the DMC; identifying relevant policies and priorities of the DMC governments, civil society, and other stakeholders; and using these data and relevant policies and priorities as a basis for the CPS. This process also helps determine the GESI results indicators for monitoring.

(iv) **Design and monitoring framework.** This is ADB's main tool for managing program and project development results and a core element of ADB's project performance management system.[20] A project's gender categorization depends on the extent to which gender-related targets and performance indicators are integrated into its DMF (footnote 16). The DMF presents the project's GESI-related impact, outcomes, outputs, and performance targets and indicators. It provides the project teams with a framework to monitor and evaluate the project's GESI development results.

(v) **Gender assessment and action plan.** This is a two-part document: The first part is the gender assessment, which is required for all ADB operations. It describes the gender equality issues and the relevance of proposed gender actions to the project. The second part is the gender action plan for GEN- and EGM-categorized projects (footnote 16). A gender action plan incorporates (a) gender performance indicators of the project DMF; (b) additional gender performance indicators that will help achieve the project's gender-related objectives and targets; and (c) activities, resources, responsibilities, and timelines for implementation and monitoring.[21] SARD uses a GESI action plan (rather than a GAP) to include activities and targets for the social inclusion of other disadvantaged groups in project areas.

[16] ADB has a four-tier gender categorization system, which defines the extent of gender features in a project design. At the highest level is the gender equity theme (GEN) category, where the project's design and monitoring framework (DMF) has at least one gender performance indicator at the outcome level and at least one gender performance indicator in 50% of the DMF outputs. Next to GEN is effective gender mainstreaming (EGM), which is not required to have a gender indicator at the outcome level but should have at least one gender indicator in 50% of the DMF outputs. Each project categorized GEN and EGM, except for results-based or policy-based loans, is required to have a gender action plan (called a GESI action plan in SARD). The gender category after EGM is some gender elements (SGE), which has gender indicators in less than 50% of the DMF outputs. The last gender category is no gender elements, which has no gender performance indicators in the DMF. All projects, including those that are categorized no gender elements, are required to integrate gender considerations in the project's social safeguards framework and/or plan. ADB. 2021. Guidelines for Gender Mainstreaming Categories of ADB Projects. Manila.

[17] ADB. Country Planning Documents: Strategies and Operations Business Plans.

[18] ADB. 2012. *Handbook on Poverty and Social Analysis: A Working Document*. Manila. This handbook provides guides for conducting a country gender assessment for a CPS.

[19] ADB's Corporate Results Framework and gender mainstreaming guidelines require the disaggregation of data by sex (male-female); however, in South Asia, particularly in four DMCs (Bangladesh. Bhutan, India, and Nepal), which legally define gender identity as non-binary, data disaggregation may go beyond the binary sex (male-female).

[20] ADB. 2020. *Guidelines for Preparing and Using a Design and Monitoring Framework: Sovereign Operations and Technical Assistance*. Manila. p. 1.

[21] ADB. 2023. Staff Instruction for Promoting Gender Equality and Women's Empowerment in ADB Operations. Manila. This staff instruction is based on the Operations Manual section on gender equality and women's empowerment in ADB operations (OM C2, issued on 30 June 2023) and the documents cited therein.

B.   ADB's Mechanisms for Evaluating and Reporting the Gender Equality and Social Inclusion Results of Operations

11.   ADB reports the GESI results of its operations in the following documents:

(i)   **Project completion report.** The project completion report (PCR) has gender or GESI sections in its main text that present (a) an overall description of the gender or GESI activities and targets defined in the DMF and the GAP or GESI action plan, (b) the extent to which these activities were completed and the targets achieved, (c) the resulting benefits in line with the five pillars of OP2 and three pillars OP1, and (d) the issues or challenges encountered and the lessons. The details are discussed in an appendix of the PCR. ADB has guidelines for evaluating the gender results of each project categorized *gender equity theme* or *effective gender mainstreaming* at completion.[22] The PCR undergoes a validation process by ADB's Independent Evaluation Department.[23]

(ii)   **Development Effectiveness Review.** ADB's progress in implementing Strategy 2030 is reported annually in the Development Effectiveness Review. It presents the assessment of ADB's performance against the RFIs in the corporate results framework (footnote 2). Emerging trends and actions for improving corporate performance are also presented.[24]

C.   Operational Departments' Additional Mechanisms for Evaluating Projects' Gender Equality and Social Inclusion Results

12.   To provide further evidence on the GESI impacts reported in the PCR and annual Development Effectiveness Review, the ADB operations departments, including SARD, conduct nimble or long-term impact assessment or evaluation of selected projects (box). The selection of a program or project for impact evaluation or assessment is at the discretion of each operations department.

---

[22]   ADB.2022. *Guidelines for the At-Exit Assessment of Gender Equality Results of ADB Projects.* Manila. These guidelines provide evaluation criteria and ratings for assessing project gender equality results.
[23]   ADB. Independent Evaluation Overview.
[24]   ADB. Development Effectiveness Review.

CHAPTER 3

Evaluability Assessment of a Program's or Project's Gender Equality and Social Inclusion Impacts

13.   This section provides guides on how to select programs or projects for GESI impact evaluation or assessment through project evaluability assessment. An evaluability assessment is a systematic process of determining if a program or project has high evaluability and if the impact evaluation or assessment will require a nimble or long-term approach. A project has high evaluability if it has strategic and operational relevance to ADB as determined by the presence of the five criteria listed in Table 1. The conditions for nimble evaluation and long-term evaluation are in the box.

Table 1: High or Low Project Gender Equality and Social Inclusion Evaluability

Criterion
1. The program's or project's design and monitoring framework has GESI outcome indicators.
2. The program's or project's GESI outcome indicators are related to ADB's corporate results framework tracking indicators for Strategy 2030 OP1 and OP2.
3. The project interventions directly or indirectly address the GESI needs of women, men, older people, people with disabilities, minority social identity groups, people with diverse SOGIESC, income poor, or other people experiencing discrimination because of their intersecting disadvantaged identities.
4. There is a lack of recent (5 years or less) empirical studies in the DMCs that attribute the achievement of GESI results to intervention(s) related to the program or project or describe the perspectives of project beneficiaries on the project interventions and their results.
5. Similar programs and projects are in ADB SARD's pipeline.

ADB = Asian Development Bank; DMC = developing member country; GESI = gender equality and social inclusion; OP1 = operational priority 1; OP2 = operational priority 2; SARD = South Asia Department; SOGIESC = sexual orientation, gender identity and expression, and sex characteristics.

Note: A program or project has high evaluability if at least the first four criteria are true.

Source: Asian Development Bank (South Asia Department).

14.   An evaluability assessment should take place at the project design phase when there is time to (i) include the GESI impact evaluation (if deemed needed) in the DMF's list of data sources or means for verifying the achievement of the GESI outcome indicators, and (ii) incorporate adequate budget in the project's total cost. Identifying the need for GESI impact evaluation at project onset can also ensure the systematic gathering of needed baseline or pre-project data. However, there are cases when the high evaluability of a program and/or project becomes more apparent during implementation or at completion. At that project phase, the collection of baseline data is too late. However, in place of an impact evaluation, an impact assessment may be done.

15.　　　If a program or project is assessed to have high evaluability, the next step is deciding who will do the impact evaluation or assessment. If a long-term evaluation or assessment is required, or the internal resources (staff time and competency) are inadequate to conduct a nimble evaluation or assessment, then SARD's GESI team and the project team or the partner executing and/or implementing agency may engage a GESI impact evaluation or assessment consulting firm. Whether nimble or long-term or in-house or outsourced, the GESI impact evaluation can engage the project target beneficiaries, especially those mentioned in para. 4, not only as sources of data but also as participants in defining the purpose and methods of GESI impact evaluation, collecting and collating the data, and analyzing the collated data and its implications.

CHAPTER 4
Guides for Evaluating or Assessing the Gender Equality and Social Inclusion Impacts of Operations

16.   Broadly, the impact evaluation or assessment process can be divided into different steps: (i) defining the evaluation or assessment framework and questions; (ii) determining what type of data to collect based on the framework and questions; (iii) defining the evaluation or assessment design based on the questions and type of data to collect; (iv) designing the sampling and data collection, collation, and analysis methods; and (v) conducting the evaluation and analyzing, reporting, and disseminating the results. Familiarity with the three general evaluation and assessment methods (quantitative, qualitative, and mixed methods) is important in designing and undertaking these steps. Generally, the quantitative and qualitative methods have different ways of conducting these steps but may be mixed to bring to the surface a more comprehensive understanding of a program's or project's GESI impacts. This section describes these differences and how to use quantitative, qualitative, or mixed methods for GESI impact evaluation.

A.   Defining the Framework of a Gender Equality and Social Inclusion Impact Evaluation or Assessment

17.   The GESI impact evaluation or assessment framework refers to the evaluation or assessment's proposition, which, in general, is that the project interventions have impacts on the targeted beneficiaries. The details of the framework may be articulated or illustrated in the project's theory of change or results chain—i.e., a project's key activities or interventions are expected to result in the targeted outputs, these outputs are expected to lead to the achievement of the outcomes, and these outcomes will lead to the realization of the envisaged impact—that is defined in the program's or project's DMF.[25] The figure presents an example of a theory of change used for the impact evaluation of the ADB-financed Madhya Pradesh Energy Efficiency Improvement Investment Program.

18.   While both quantitative and qualitative methods may illustrate their proposition in a theory of change, the foci of their investigation differ. The quantitative method examines the statistical significance of the cause-and-effect relation of the variables (e.g., presented in boxes in the figure) and, therefore, represents the variable in each box in numerical form (e.g., data in ordinal or interval or ratio form; and nominal and categorical data transformed into dummy variables for statistical analysis). Conversely, the qualitative method examines more the perception or understanding of the project beneficiaries, especially women, men, and people with diverse SOGIESC belonging to disadvantaged groups, on the variable in each box—i.e., a project's inputs, outputs, outcomes, and impacts—and how this understanding is affected by their situational context and perspective on the project proponent (e.g., ADB and the executing and/or implementing agency). Therefore, it represents the variable in each box in qualitative form (e.g., stories, answers to open-ended questions, observations, visuals, transcripts of conversations). However,

---

[25]   For further guidance on the theory of change and how to prepare it, refer to H. White and D. A. Raitzer. 2017. *Impact Evaluation of Development Interventions: A Practical Guide.* Manila: ADB (Chapter 2). pp. 20–30.

unlike the quantitative method, the qualitative method does not need to start with these variables. Instead, the questioning could begin with an open-ended question or a request for the participants to share their stories about their experience with the project, its results, and project proponents.

Quantitative Method

19.   The quantitative method explains the theory of change in the form of hypothesized causal linkages or correlation of variables, i.e., project interventions or treatment, outputs, outcomes, and impact. Overall, the hypothesis of a GESI impact evaluation is that the GESI-related improvements in the project areas and the situation of project beneficiaries, particularly women and excluded and vulnerable groups, can be attributed to the project interventions. To strengthen the plausibility of this hypothesis, the evaluator may present supporting related studies. This method uses long-established statistical measurements for (i) analyzing the reliability of data collection instruments; (ii) identifying the adequate number of samples; (iii) examining the statistical significance of the differences of the treatment and comparison groups of samples, including the margin of error; (iv) checking the internal and external validity of findings; and (v) verifying the presence or absence of causal linkages between the project interventions and GESI-related outcomes in project areas.

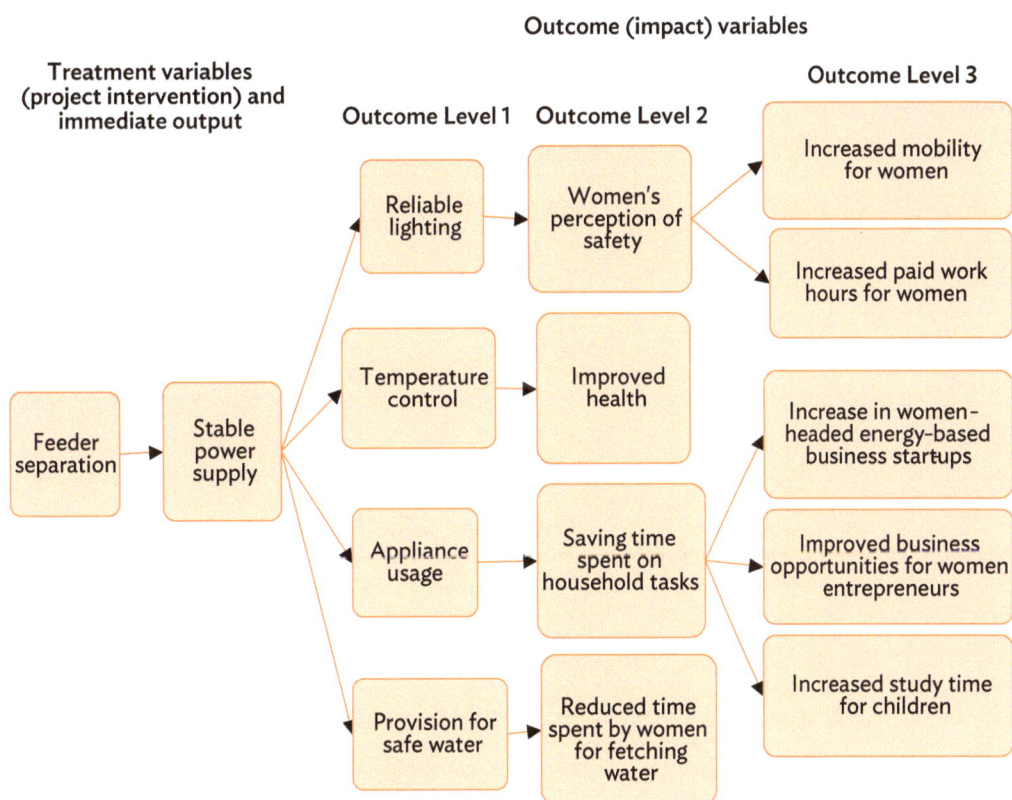

Figure: Theory of Change of the Impact Evaluation of Improved Electricity Supply and Access

Source: Asian Development Bank.

Qualitative Method

20.   As mentioned in para. 5, the proponents of qualitative methods argue that quantitative methods tend to miss (i) the subjective meanings that respondents give to their answers to structured questions, (ii) the social and gender context of answers, and (iii) the way the respondents position the project proponent or evaluator (footnote 8). Hence, the qualitative impact evaluation framework is defined along these three lines. For GESI impact evaluations, the proposition is that the project's GESI impacts can be best identified and understood by examining the shared (and discordant) meanings that women, men, and people with diverse SOGIESC, especially those belonging to disadvantaged groups, give to the project's purpose and results, and how these meanings are affected by their social and gender contexts and their perception of the motivation or interests of the project proponents (e.g., ADB and the executing and/or implementing agency). In addition, some methodologies, such as the most significant change technique, have been specifically developed and used for this purpose.[26] The evaluator may do a review of related studies. However, the findings of the studies will be used not as a basis of a hypothesis but as context knowledge to understand the participants' statements and/or behavior.[27]

Mixed Methods

21.   Though quantitative and qualitative methods come from different worldviews, they can be mixed for pragmatic purposes.[28] This means that the evaluator can combine the practical uses of quantitative and qualitative methods to conduct in-depth analysis of the project's GESI impacts.[29] This mixture implies more work and more cost, but doing so could give the evaluator a better understanding or broader view of the project's GESI impacts. If adequate resources (time and funds) are unavailable, the evaluator may have to choose which one better serves the purpose of the impact evaluation. Overall, the factors to consider in deciding whether to use quantitative or qualitative or mixed methods, especially if applied in social and gender relations studies, such as the GESI impacts of project interventions, include the type of data to collect and the importance of considering the context of the data.[30]

---

[26] The most significant change technique a qualitative monitoring and evaluation technique also used for impact evaluation that was developed in Bangladesh in the 1990s. The technique has additional reasons for using a qualitative impact evaluation method. According to Rick Davies, its author, the technique, which involves the collection of stories of change by project stakeholders, is most useful when (i) it is not possible to predict in any detail or with certainty the outcomes of the project, (ii) outcomes vary widely across beneficiaries, (iii) stakeholders do not agree on the most important outcomes, and (iv) interventions are expected to be participatory. For guidance on how to use the most significant change technique, refer to Intrac. 2017. *Most Significant Change*.

[27] Footnote 8, p. 49.

[28] A. Tashakkori and C. Teddlie, eds. 2010. *SAGE Handbook of Mixed Methods in Social and Behavioral Research*. Second Edition. Thousand Oaks, California, United States: SAGE Publications.

[29] In the simultaneous use of quantitative and qualitative methods (i.e., simultaneous data collection—when the interview guide contains both quantitative and qualitative questions—and analysis), the evaluator needs to identity the dominant method, whose theoretical drive will be followed. For instance, if the dominant method is quantitative, the theoretical drive is quantitative (i.e., hypothesis testing) and the qualitative part is supplementary. J. Morse. 2010. Procedures and Practice of Mixed Methods Design. In A. Tashakkori and C. Teddlie, eds. *SAGE Handbook of Mixed Methods in Social and Behavioral Research*. Second Edition. Thousand Oaks, California, United States: SAGE Publications.

[30] S. Garbarino and J. Holland. 2009. *Quantitative and Qualitative Methods in Impact Evaluation and Measuring Results: Issues Paper*. This issues paper was commissioned by the UK Department of International Development (DFID) through the Emerging Issues Research Service of the Governance and Social Development Resource Centre (GSDRC).

B.   Formulation of the Evaluation Questions and Types of Data to Collect and Analyze

Quantitative Method

22.   Based on the impact evaluation's theory of change, the evaluator formulates the evaluation or assessment question(s) and the types of data to collect. For instance, for the theory of change in Figure 4.1, the questions are on the causal relations of the variables, such as the following:

(i)   What is the effect of the feeder separation program (cause) on the households' level of power supply (effect) in project areas?

(ii)   Has the improved power supply (cause) led to reliable lighting, ability to control temperature, use of electric appliances, and accessibility of safe water (effects)?

(iii)   Has reliable lighting (cause) affected women's perception of safety (effect)? Has women's perception of safety affected women's mobility and work hours (effects)?

23.   To do a quantitative or statistical analysis of the causal relations of variables or attribution analysis, the data on each variable should be in numerical form: (i) households' level of power supply (hours a day), (ii) reliability of households' lighting (hours a day), (iii) temperature control (number of households with devices for heating or cooling), (iv) access to water (number of households with easy access to safe water), (v) women's perception of safety (measured using a scale), (vi) improved health (number households with members who got sick in a specified period), (vii) time spent by women versus men in household tasks (hours a day), (viii) number of new women-headed energy-based businesses, (ix) number of new business opportunities for women entrepreneurs, and (x) children's study time (hours a day).

Qualitative Methods

24.   In a qualitative impact evaluation, the questions seek to determine the meanings that the respondents give on the project and its results and how these meanings are influenced by their situational context and their perceived motivation or interest of the project proponent and/or evaluator. Examples of questions are as follows:

(i)   What are the narratives of women, men, and people with diverse SOGIESC of disadvantaged groups (including community- or identity-based organizations and nongovernment organizations) about the project and its outcomes on women, men, girls, boys, people with diverse SOGIESC (especially to those belonging to disadvantaged groups) in the project areas?

    a.   What do these narratives say about the meanings they give to the project and its results, given the social and gender context in the project areas?

    b.   In these narratives, how do they position ADB and the executing and/or implementing agency (e.g., as champions of poverty reduction and GESI, as agents or protectors of capitalist interests, or others)? What are their bases for this positioning of ADB and the executing and/or implementing agency? How do they position themselves (e.g., active participants, passive beneficiaries, non-beneficiaries) in relation to the project? How do they describe their own stake and ownership of the project and its results? Do they think they had adequate agency and voice to ensure that the project benefits them too?

(ii) What are the similar and different views of women, men, girls, boys, and people with diverse SOGIESC on the most significant changes brought about by the project and on the project's approaches that worked and did not work? What are their recommendations for future projects?

25. These questions are answered by collecting and analyzing the beneficiaries' stories, discourses or conversations, answers to open-ended questions, and nonverbal messages (behavior) about the project, its GESI results, and the project proponents, which are all qualitative data.

C. Defining the Impact Evaluation or Assessment Design

26. The types of questions to ask and the requirements to answer these questions will determine the GESI impact evaluation design. Examples of quantitative and qualitative evaluation designs for GESI impact evaluation or assessment are in Table 2.

Table 2: Impact Evaluation Designs

Impact Evaluation Design	General Description or Requirements
I. QUANTITATIVE ANALYSIS OF THE RELATION OF TWO OR MORE VARIABLES	
A. Experimental design • Randomized control trials	1. The evaluation question entails comparing two types of groups: reference group (sample of targeted project beneficiaries) and comparison group (sample of people in non-project areas) before project implementation and after project completion. 2. Members of the reference and comparison groups are randomly assigned—random assignment (e.g., through drawing of lots) means that all members of a selected population have an equal chance to be part of the reference or comparison groups; this also means that project intervention or services will be given only to those who are randomly assigned to the reference group. 3. Members of reference and comparison groups serve as a representative sample of the population, which is required for the generalization of evaluation results or general application of the evaluation findings; this may require a large sample size. 4. Collection of pre- and post-project data on the reference and comparison groups.
B. Nonexperimental design • Quasi-experimental design	1. The evaluation question also entails comparing two groups (the same as in experimental design). However, a random assignment of sample participants or respondents to the reference and comparison groups is not feasible because of cost and/or ethical reasons (e.g., services to those in the comparison group cannot be withheld or delayed for the purpose of the impact evaluation or experiment). 2. Baseline or pre-project data are unavailable; hence, pre- and post-project comparison of the reference and comparison groups is not possible. 3. Members of reference and comparison groups serve as a representative sample of the population, which is required for the generalization of evaluation results or general application of the evaluation findings; this may require a large sample size. 4. The comparison group should have the same characteristics as the reference group except for the project intervention.

continued on next page

Table 2 continued

Impact Evaluation Design	General Description or Requirements
II. QUALITATIVE ANALYSIS OF QUALITATIVE DATA	
A. Phenomenology • Description of experiences of individuals or groups B. Narrative analysis • Description and analysis of stories of individuals and groups	1. The evaluation entails collecting information and stories about the experience of women, men, girls, boys, and people with diverse SOGIESC (especially those belonging to disadvantaged groups) in the project and its results. 2. Purposive selection of participants—based on selection criteria relevant to the evaluation. For example, members of disadvantaged groups that are targeted to benefit from the project with significant representation of women, men, and people with diverse SOGIESC (para. 32 of the main text). If the social or political environment does not allow people with diverse SOGIESC to overtly participate without fear or harm, then caution should be observed in identifying and interviewing them. 3. In-depth interviews with participants (individual and/or focus group discussions). 4. Small number of samples for in-depth qualitative analysis of rich qualitative data. 5. Findings describe the participants of the study, not the whole population. 6. The participants should confirm or validate the results through, for instance, consultation workshops. The findings validation process may involve other project beneficiaries who did not participate in the evaluation.
C. Ethnography • Description and analysis of culture (e.g., social and gender norms)	1. The evaluation question entails collecting stories and observing change(s) in practices and behavior of people (women, men, girls, boys, and people with diverse SOGIESC, including those from disadvantaged groups); families; communities; organizations; and service providers in the project areas. 2. Purposive selection of participants (based on criteria relevant to the evaluation). 3. In-depth interviews, focus group discussions, and direct observation of the subjects or participants and their interactions in their natural setting. 4. Small number of samples for in-depth qualitative analysis of rich qualitative data. 5. Participants should confirm or validate the results through, for instance, consultation workshops. The findings validation process may involve other project beneficiaries who did not participate in the evaluation.

SOGIESC = sexual orientation, gender identity and expressions, and sex characteristics.
Sources: H. White and D. A. Raitzer. 2017. *Impact Evaluation of Development Interventions: A Practical Guide.* Manila: ADB; and U. Flick. 2009. *An Introduction to Qualitative Research.* Fourth Edition. London: SAGE Publications.

27.   The impact evaluation may employ a mixed qualitative and quantitative method design, which is a combination of one quantitative method and at least one qualitative method in Table 2 (or other methods, because the list in Table 2 is not exhaustive).

28.   Apart from the impact evaluation design, another decision to make based on the evaluation questions is the unit of analysis, which will be the basis for the selection of participants.

(i)   Will the analysis focus on individuals, e.g., women, men, people with disability, people with diverse SOGIESC, older people, or persons experiencing overlapping discrimination because of their intersecting disadvantaged identities?

(ii)   Will the analysis focus on households, e.g., women-headed households (not only the woman head but the household she heads) versus men-headed households?

(iii)   Will the analysis focus on communities, e.g., communities of disadvantaged ethnic groups?

D. Designing the Methods for Selection of Samples

29.   This section provides the general points to consider when designing the methods for selecting the participants of the GESI impact evaluation.

Quantitative Method

30.   In a quantitative method, the generalization of results (to the population where the samples were drawn) is important. This means that the findings on the select number of samples (e.g., 500 women in project areas) should describe the whole population of the study (e.g., 5,000 women in project areas). Hence, systematic procedures for selecting a set of samples representative of the population are important. Three points are crucial to consider in the selection of samples for a quantitative evaluation of GESI impacts: [31]

   (i)   **Defining the population frame.** This refers to—depending on the unit of analysis—all individuals, households, or groups on whom or on which the GESI impact evaluation focuses.
   (ii) **Number of samples that is a representative sample of the defined population.** The general rule is that the larger the sample, the more likely it is representative of the population, and the more powerful the statistical analysis (i.e., the probability of committing an error is less). However, the allocated funds may not be enough for a large sample. Hence, a careful calculation of the minimum sufficient number of samples is important to avoid committing a statistical error. The evaluator will need the assistance of an expert in statistical analysis to compute the appropriate sample size.
   (iii) **Method for selecting the participants.** A careful and systematic procedure is needed to avoid biased samples and ensure that the selected participants serve as a representative sample of the population. The general rule is a random selection, where each person in the defined population frame has an equal chance of being selected as a participant in the study, which can avoid bias in selecting samples.

31.   In a quasi-experimental design, the comparison group should have the same characteristics as the reference group, except for the project intervention. Hence, their selection should also be systematic to avoid the effects of extraneous (uncontrolled, irrelevant) variables on the statistical analysis of data. One way is to use propensity score matching so that the members of the comparison group match those in the reference group.[32]

Qualitative Method

32.   Qualitative GESI impact evaluation does not aim for the generalization of results. Hence, its sample size is not as strict as that in quantitative research and is typically smaller. The suggestions of research experts range from 5 to 50 samples for qualitative studies that aim to describe experiences.[33] The number of samples will depend on the (i) types of people or households or groups or communities being studied; (ii) level of data saturation, which means that no additional stories or experiences or feedback on the project's impacts are emerging; and (iii) available resources. Generally, a small sample size per type of people, household, or group is preferred for an

---

[31]   For guidance in determining sample size and sampling method, refer to H. White and D. A. Raitzer. 2017. *Impact Evaluation of Development Interventions: A Practical Guide.* Manila. (Chapter 7 and Appendix 2).
[32]   Propensity score matching is a quasi-experimental method in which the researcher uses statistical techniques to construct an artificial control group by matching each treated unit with a non-treated unit of similar characteristics. World Bank. DIME Wiki. Propensity Score Matching.
[33]   M. Moran. 2013. *Qualitative Sample Size.* Statistics Solutions. 4 September.

in-depth qualitative study. The purposive sampling method—through the use of a set of criteria—is used to select the participants. The following are some suggestions for the selection of samples using the purposive method:[34]

(i) **Purposive selection of extreme cases (which can appear in a quantitative method as outliers).** The extreme cases could be project beneficiaries whom key informants report as experiencing large benefits in terms of income increase and positive changes in community participation and leadership skills. They could also be those who show a lack of progress.

(ii) **Purposive selection of typical cases.** They are project beneficiaries whom key informants describe as not extreme cases and appear to represent the majority of project beneficiaries.

(iii) **Purposive selection for maximal variation of the participants.** Typical cases (and extreme cases, if any) for each type of group (e.g., gender, age range, SOGIESC, ethnic group, with and without disabilities) and those experiencing overlapping discrimination because of their multiple intersecting disadvantaged identities (e.g., income poor older women or youth with disabilities who are members of excluded and vulnerable ethnic groups) could be selected to ensure representation of different types of groups of project beneficiaries.

(iv) **Convenience sampling.** This refers to the selection of participants that are easiest to access (those immediately available) under given conditions, such as following disaster triggered by natural hazards or armed conflict, or if this is the only way to do the evaluation given limited time and resources (e.g., community visits during ADB missions for the preparation of the project completion report).

33. If children (below age 18) will be among the selected sample beneficiaries, in conformity with the International Charter for Ethical Research Involving Children, it is important to seek the children's parent(s) or guardian(s) written or verbal consent. The children should also be made aware that they may back out anytime from the study or choose not to answer the questions if they are not ready.[35]

E. Data Sources or Collection Methods

34. Both quantitative and qualitative methods use primary and secondary data. Primary data refers to first-hand data collected by the evaluator directly from the project beneficiaries. In contrast, secondary data refers to data collected in the past, such as in studies or project operations. Examples of primary data are key informant interviews, surveys, observations, and visuals; and examples of secondary data are available and accessible government statistical and administrative data, project reports, and news reports.

Quantitative Method

35. Sources of data for quantitative impact evaluation include censuses; surveys; geographic information systems; remote sensing; administrative data; and other sources of real-time data, such as devices that record traffic flows, pollution levels, and others.[36] Most of the questions in a survey instrument ask participants to select from multiple answers, pre-coded for easier entry in a data table and statistical analysis. If collected qualitative data are included in the statistical analysis, they are summarized, coded, and transformed into quantitative form.

---

[34] Footnote 8, p. 122.

[35] A. Graham et al. 2013. *Ethical Research Involving Children.* Florence: United Nations Children's Fund (UNICEF) Office of Research-Innocenti.

[36] H. White and D. A. Raitzer. 2017. *Impact Evaluation of Development Interventions: A Practical Guide.* Manila: ADB. This ADB material also provides guides for preparing a survey instrument, including the designing of specific questions.

Categorical data, such as gender, ethnicity, disability, and types of benefits received, are converted into numeric variables (called dummy variables) for entry in the statistical analysis equation.

Qualitative Method

36.   Qualitative impact evaluation uses open-ended and unstructured questions. Unlike closed questions, which are answerable by "yes," "no," "I don't know," or "not applicable," open-ended questions (e.g., what, why, how, when) allow the respondent to give any answers and to elaborate. Unstructured questions, unlike structured questions, have no prepared list of answers from which the respondent can choose.

37.   The selection of data sources will depend on the purpose or focus of the GESI impact evaluation and available resources (time and evaluator[s]). Examples of qualitative data sources are in Table 3.

Table 3: Qualitative Data Sources

Type of Data	Data Source
1. Verbal data	1. Focused interview using a questionnaire with open-ended, unstructured questions. 2. Focus group discussion (6 to 8 participants) with open-ended or unstructured guide questions to be held from 0.5 to 2 hours. This is used when part of the objective is to identify shared group opinions and areas of disagreement, and if the evaluator expects the participants to be willing to share their thoughts, feelings, and apprehensions in the presence of others. 3. Narrative interview using a "generative narrative question" that intends to stimulate the interviewee's narration of all events related to the project from its beginning to end (e.g., "Please share your experience with the project. The best way is to start from when you learned about the project.") Narrative probing may be given to fill in some narrative gaps. At the last stage, the interviewer may ask about the participant's reflections, feelings, lessons, and assessment of her or his experience in the project and the benefits.
2. Observation	4. Participant observation, in which the evaluator goes to the project area(s) to directly observe the practices and interactions of people in their everyday life situations and settings. The focus of observation depends on the project's impacts under investigation, e.g., who has access to electricity and for what purpose(s) is it used by women, men, and people with diverse SOGIESC? How do children go to school? What are the daily activities of women compared to men? Who speaks and makes decisions during community meetings? Participant observation may include unstructured interviews to clarify observed practices.
3. Visual data	5. Photos, videos, and films (if available) that depict the situation in the project areas before and after the project. The use of visual data shows how the camera can be used as an instrument for collecting qualitative data. These visual data could be used during focus group discussions to stimulate group reflections and assessment of project impacts and processes, and to validate the representativeness of the visuals about the situation in the areas before and after the project.
4. Documents	6. Documents include project reports, annual reports, e-mails or letters, diaries or journals, laws, and policies developed through the project.

SOGIESC = sexual orientation, gender identity and expression, and sex characteristics.

Source: U. Flick. 2009. *An Introduction to Qualitative Research*. Fourth Edition. London: SAGE Publications.

38.   It is essential to reiterate (as mentioned in para. 15) that, in a qualitative method, the project beneficiaries can participate actively as the source of data and as data collectors and analysts. Therefore, if a participatory GESI impact evaluation or assessment is done, the lead evaluator must select a manageable number of project beneficiaries to train as evaluators. The training would be on how to define the purpose of the GESI impact

evaluation, collect and analyze qualitative data, and facilitate focus group or community discussions. Through this process, the GESI impact evaluation or assessment also becomes a strategy for organizing the community and developing the capacity of the community to sustain and expand the project's gains.

F.   Data Collation

39.   Data collation refers to the process of organizing all collected data in one file in a way that makes them ready for analysis, whether for statistical or qualitative analysis. In both quantitative and qualitative methods, the general practice is to observe the rule of confidentiality of the sources of data. Hence, the names of the participants should not appear in the data collation tables and the report.

Quantitative Method

40.   In quantitative impact evaluation, the data are numeric (Table 4). Qualitative answers to open-ended questions in the survey questionnaire are pre-coded and converted into dummy variables and entered into the data table in numeric form. For example, for evaluations that examine the project impacts on different gender identities, sexual orientations, and ethnic groups, the analysis could have gender identity variable, sexual orientation variable, and ethnic group varibable. For the gender identity variable, the data could be coded 1 for cisgender man, 2 for cisgender woman, 3 for transgender man, 4 for transgender women, or 5 for other nonbinary individuals. For the sexual orientation variable, the data could be coded 1 for straight or heterosexual, 2 for same-sex attracted, or 3 for bisexual or attracted to both sexes). For the ethnicity variable, each ethnic group is given a numeric code. Hence, at the data collation phase, all data about and from each participant or sample are expected to be ready to be transferred in a data table, which can be in a Microsoft Excel file or directly in the data table of the statistical software (e.g., Stata, SPSS).

Table 4: An Example of Dataset for Statistical Analysis

Respondent[a]	Gender Identity[b]	Sexual Orientation[c]	Ethnic Group[d]	Household Chores (hours per day)	Income[e] ($)	Savings[f] ($)	Safety[g]	Leader[h]
1	2	3	3	4	950	150	3	1
2	1	2	4	2	600	75	5	2
3	4	1	2	3	800	50	4	2
4	3	2	1	3	600	45	3	1

[a] Respondents' names are numerically coded for identification.
[b] Gender Identity = 1 if respondent is a cisgender man, 2 if a cisgender woman, 3 if a transgender man, and 4 if a transgender woman.
[c] Sexual orientation = 1 if heterosexual, 2 if homosexual, and 3 if bisexual or attracted to both sexes.
[d] Number code assigned to a respondent's ethnic group.
[e] Average monthly income.
[f] Average monthly savings.
[g] Perception of safety outside of the home on a scale of 1 to 5, with 5 = "very safe" and 1 = "not very safe."
[h] Leader = 2 if a voting member of the leadership body of a community-based organization, and 1 if not.

Source: Asian Development Bank (South Asia Department).

41.   The process of entering the data in the statistical software includes labeling the type of data of each variable. The two most common data are numeric (e.g., income, savings, hours, perception of safety on a scale) and string or categorical (e.g., gender, ethnicity, membership in a leadership body, disability).

Qualitative Method

42.   In qualitative impact evaluation, the collation of answers to open-ended questions begins with separating the statements (sentences, phrases, or paragraphs) of each participant, or in observation reports that appear to have different themes, and inputting these statements in a data table (Table 5). The qualitative data can be organized in a Microsoft Excel file or Microsoft Word table, or imported into the data section of qualitative data analysis software (e.g., NVivo). It would be better to use a software program like NVivo as it accepts visual data and facilitates the identification and analysis of the data themes and subthemes.

Table 5: An Example of Dataset for Qualitative Analysis (When Microsoft Excel or Word Is Used)

Respondent[a]	Gender[b]	Ethnic Group[c]	Participant's Statement During the Interview or Focus Group Discussion	Theme[d]
1	2	3	"Before the project, we had no source of income to support our children's health care needs and school fees and buy nutritious food and clothing."	A
1	2	3	"The project supported us with a 2-day training on vegetable farming. But we had no irrigation facility. We discussed this problem with the project team. As a result, they helped build a water pond in our village."	B
1	2	3	"With the water problem resolved, I can plant vegetables like onions, garlic, ladyfingers, chilies, cauliflower, cucumber, tomatoes, radish, and carrots. I also applied the knowledge, skills, and techniques for vegetable farming learned from the training. Now, I earn NRs6,000 per month by selling the vegetables."	C

[a] Respondents' names are numerically coded for identification.

[b] Gender = 1 if respondent is a cisgender man, 2 if a cisgender woman, 3 if a transgender man, and 4 if a transgender woman.

[c] Number code assigned to a respondent's ethnic group.

[d] The codes for the first level of thematic analysis, e.g., A is about problems before project intervention, B is about the support received from the project, and C is about the benefits experienced. The second level is identifying the subthemes of the statements (e.g., types of problems, types of support, and types of benefits).

Notes: The entry of statements will be done for all participants or respondents. When all statements have been entered, they are sorted by the "Theme" column, which will group all statements with the same themes together for easier further analysis.

Source: Asian Development Bank (South Asia Department).

43.   The complete dataset is a vital resource for the impact evaluation as it puts together all data collected from the participants and is the basis of the impact evaluation findings. Hence, careful attention should be given to the accurate entry of the collected data into this table. It is also important to keep a copy (and to require the consulting firm to submit a copy), as it may be used for other research work of ADB.

G. Data Analysis

Quantitative Method

44.   For quantitative impact evaluation or assessment, selecting the appropriate statistical method to use and the statistical analysis of the collated data will require an expert in statistical analysis, whether using Stata, SPSS, or other software. In general, the analysis of the difference between pre-project and post-project data will require a statistical analysis of longitudinal data. These methods include the difference-in-differences and fixed effects model in Stata (footnote 36). Another method is fixed effects regression for repeated measures (longitudinal data) in SPSS. If baseline or pre-project data are absent and the comparison is between the reference and comparison groups in their post-project condition only, then the appropriate statistical method will depend on the number and types of treatment variables and outcome variables. An expert in statistical analysis can guide the selection and use of the appropriate statistical method and interpretation of the results. These results will be the basis for confirming or disconfirming the hypotheses of the GESI impact evaluation.

Qualitative Method

45.   For qualitative impact evaluation or assessment, the best method, as mentioned in para. 42, is to use qualitative data analysis software, such as NVivo, for easier and better data analysis. However, the use of this software requires an expert in this software. In the absence of an expert, an alternative is to do the analysis manually, such as cutting and sorting the statements (as indicated in para. 42 and Table 5) until all themes and subthemes of the qualitative data (e.g., verbal data, participant observation report, visual data, and available documents) are identified. In this analysis, the evaluator needs to have in mind two general types of themes: those coming from the evaluation questions and those coming from the participants.[37] The themes and/or subthemes coming from the participants may be said in indigenous typologies, metaphors, or proverbs unfamiliar to the evaluator. In this situation, the evaluator needs to return to the participants or informants for additional information. In participatory impact evaluation, the selected evaluators (involving women and disadvantaged groups) will participate in the identification of themes and subthemes of the collected qualitative data. The results will be presented to other members of the community for validation.

46.   When all themes and subthemes have been identified, the evaluators may further analyze these themes by looking into the following:

(i)   Frequency of mention of each theme and subtheme to identify the dominant and minority themes; this means counting the number of respondents who mentioned each theme.
(ii)   Different types of participants or beneficiaries (women, men, and people with diverse SOGIESC of disadvantaged groups) who mentioned each theme and subtheme to identity who appears to hold the dominant and minority themes and subthemes.
(iii)   Similarities and differences of the themes and subthemes to identify concordant and discordant views and who holds them (e.g., women, men, people with diverse SOGIESC of advantaged and disadvantaged groups).

---

37   G. Ryan and H. R. Bernard. 2003. Techniques to Identify Themes. *Field Methods*. 15 (1). pp. 85–109.

47.   The evaluator may also include an interpretative analysis of the possible influence of the participants' context—i.e., socioeconomic, social, and gender norms; political conditions (e.g., women's apprehensions about the repercussions of honest sharing in the presence of men or village leaders or government representatives)—and their perception of the interest of the project proponents and evaluators. It is an interpretative analysis because the evaluator articulates the evaluator's understanding of the intentions and reasons for the participants' statements or actions based on the evaluator's knowledge or available evidence of the participants' context and expectations. It is best to do this interpretative analysis through participatory methods involving the evaluation participants themselves (e.g., representatives of women, disadvantaged groups, and civil society organizations).

48.   The identified themes and subthemes of stories, answers to open-ended questions, interpretation of visual data, transcripts of discourses or conversations, and interpretation of observation reports of women and disadvantaged groups will be framed in the findings as the meanings given to the project, project results, and project proponents by the participants or data sources (i.e., women, men, and people with diverse SOGIESC of advantaged and disadvantaged groups).

H.   Discussion of Results: The Conclusion

49.   For both quantitative and qualitative GESI impact evaluation and assessment, the analysis will include the results' practical implications (i.e., the way forward or recommendations for GESI mainstreaming in similar projects) and the theoretical implications (i.e., the evaluation's contribution to the literature on GESI in South Asia). These implications are presented in the concluding part of the evaluation or assessment report. To caution the reader on the applicability of the results and overall conclusion, the evaluator also includes in the concluding section (usually presented in the beginning part of a study proposal) the limitations of the study. In qualitative GESI impact evaluation, a possible limitation is the reflexivity of the evaluators, which refers to the GESI values and attitudes or biases that they bring to the evaluation. In recognition of the role of reflexivity in the interpretation of data, evaluators should clarify the values, perspectives, and knowledge that they bring to the project's GESI impact evaluation.

CHAPTER 5

Preparing the Impact Evaluation or Assessment Report

50.   The main outline of the report for both quantitative and qualitative GESI impact evaluation or assessment is the same (Table 6).

Table 6: Points to Cover in the Gender Equality and Social Inclusion Impact Evaluation or Assessment Report

Section	Contents
Introduction	Overview of the project, results of the evaluability assessment of the project's GESI impacts, evaluation objectives, target users of the evaluation results, summary of findings of reviewed related studies, and the significance of the GESI impact evaluation.
Evaluation framework	Proposition of the impact evaluation (e.g., theory of change) and the overall GESI impact evaluation question(s).
Evaluation methods	1. GESI impact evaluation or assessment design, unit of analysis, sampling and data collection methods, profile of participants disaggregated by gender and other relevant social factors, data collation and analysis methods, and measures used to ensure the reliability of data collection instruments (interview questions or guides for focus group discussions or participant observation guides) and internal and external validity or confirmability and transferability of findings. 2. Statement if the evaluation process was participatory. If so, then this part includes (i) the profile of the evaluators (disaggregated by gender and other relevant social categories) from the project communities; their roles in the evaluation; and how they were selected, trained, and mobilized; and (ii) how the evaluation objectives, process, and results were presented to the other members—women, men, and people with diverse SOGIESC of disadvantaged groups—of the community for validation and their roles in the way forward. 3. How the impact evaluation complied with the International Charter for Ethical Research Involving Children if the participants include children (below age 18).
Analysis and results	1. Results of the analysis of data (organized according to the GESI impact evaluation questions). 2. If a quantitative method was used, include the tables of statistical analysis outputs and explanation. 3. If a qualitative method was used, include the table of themes and subthemes (framed as meanings given by the participants) of stories; answers to open-ended questions; interpretation of visual data; transcripts of conversations; and interpretation of observation reports of women, men, and people with diverse SOGIESC, especially those belonging to disadvantaged groups.
Conclusions and way forward	1. Project's GESI achievements showing GESI issues that were addressed and project's GESI-related performance indicators (as listed in the project's design and monitoring framework and GESI action plans) that were achieved. These achievements should be grouped according to the three pillars of OP1, the five pillars of OP2, and the three pillars of the LNOB framework. 2. If a quantitative method was used, state if the hypothesis or hypotheses were confirmed or not. If the hypotheses were confirmed, make an interpretative analysis of the facilitating or success factors. If the hypotheses or not all hypotheses were not confirmed, then make an interpretative analysis of the hindering factors.

continued on next page

Table 6 continued

Section	Contents
	3. If a qualitative method was used, make an interpretative analysis of the factors that may have influenced the shared and discordant meanings assigned by women, men, and people with diverse SOGIESC of disadvantaged groups to the project, its results, and the interests of ADB and executing agencies and implementing agencies, and provide reflections on the evaluation process (if participatory). 4. For both quantitative and qualitative methods, provide the evaluation's contributions to the literature on GESI in South Asia and the way forward for future similar projects and other projects in the sector to which the project belongs. Proposed actions should (i) be relevant to the objective and purposes of the evaluation, (ii) be consistent with the findings, (iii) be developed with the involvement of relevant stakeholders, (iv) clearly identify the target group for each proposed action, and (v) be grouped according to the pillars of OP1, OP2, and the LNOB framework.

ADB = Asian Development Bank; GESI = gender equality and social inclusion; LNOB = leave no one behind; OP1 = operational priority 1; OP2 = operational priority 2; SOGIESC = sexual orientation, gender identity and expression, and sex characteristics.

Source: ADB (South Asia Department).

CHAPTER 6
Dissemination Strategy

51.   SARD follows ADB's Access to Information Policy[38] and discloses evaluation findings through ADB website However, the dissemination strategy of GESI-related findings may require more approaches since some stakeholders may not have access to the ADB website because of lack of internet connection. Additionally, an interactive discussion during the dissemination process provides opportunities for future learning. Hence, it is important to design a comprehensive dissemination strategy that will efficiently distribute evaluation findings and recommendations in the most accessible, transparent, and inclusive way possible. In particular, the following should occur:

(i)   Identify and involve the participants and direct users of the evaluation. The direct users of the evaluation include the SARD project and GESI teams at ADB headquarters and resident missions, and the project's executing agency and implementing agency. Additionally, it is important to identify other stakeholders to whom the evaluation should be disseminated, how best to provide them access to information, and how to engage them in disseminating the findings.

(ii)   Identify potential users who may benefit from the evaluation findings or may be interested in the evaluation's or assessment's conclusions. These may include international and national human rights groups, women's rights and gender equality groups, identity-based organizations, and other civil society organizations; duty bearers and their government counterparts (at the national and local levels).

(iii)   Provide barrier-free access to evaluation products. This entails ensuring that the report language and format are accessible to all potential users. The version of the report to be disseminated should be written in clear and understandable language to meet the demand and needs of its potential audience. In particular, the report—or at least its summary—should be translated into the local language(s).

(iv)   Use targeted GESI-responsive knowledge products to reduce barriers to information and sharing of lessons learned and experiences. Such products may include the dissemination of lessons learned and best practices. Seeking alternative ways to present the evaluation findings to excluded and vulnerable groups is essential and fulfills their right to know the conclusions of a study that concerns them.

(v)   Develop evaluation products that use alternative ways of depicting information (e.g., through imagery, theatre, poetry, music, and infographics). Involve media outlets in the dissemination phase. Social media channels can also be an effective means to make the findings more engaging and to share evaluation results with traditionally unreached audiences and communities. Select the most appropriate dissemination product for each group. The choice between various products will also depend on the human and financial resources available.

---

[38]   ADB. 2018. *Access to Information Policy*. Manila.

CHAPTER 7
Conclusions

52.   For GESI impact evaluation or assessment, the best option is to engage an expert GESI impact evaluation or assessment team, especially when the results of the project GESI evaluability assessment show the need for long-term evaluation or when SARD uses the evaluation or assessment as a strategy for organizing and developing the capacity of the project communities to sustain the project's gains. For the quantitative method, expertise is particularly needed for the computation of appropriate sample size, preparation of survey instruments, training of enumerators or interviewers, selection and running of the appropriate statistical method, and interpretation of the statistical results. For the qualitative method, expertise is needed for the description of the framework and the appropriate selection and rigorous use of data collection methods (e.g., interviewing, facilitation of focus group discussions, camera use, participant observation, and review of documents); the use of the qualitative data analysis software (e.g., NVivo); and interpretative data analysis. If participatory GESI impact evaluation or assessment will be employed, then expertise in selecting and training a core group of evaluators among the project beneficiaries and mobilizing community participation in the evaluation or assessment process is also needed. There are nongovernment organizations that are well trained and experienced to conduct participatory action research or participatory GESI impact evaluation or assessment. Overall, the power of the GESI impact evaluation or assessment results also relies on the credibility and expertise of the evaluators.

Appendixes

Appendix 1: Gender Equality and Social Inclusion Impact Evaluation Questions Based on the Pillars of Operational Priorities 1 and 2

Pillars of Strategy 2030 Operational Priorities 1 and 2 and Intersectionality	Areas for Gender Equality and Social Inclusion Impact Evaluation		
	Understand for Action	Empower for Change	Include for Opportunity
OP1 (addressing remaining poverty and reducing inequalities) pillars: 1. Human capital and social protection enhanced for all 2. Quality jobs generated 3. Opportunities for the most vulnerable increased	1. Did the project aim to benefit the excluded and vulnerable groups in project areas? If yes, who are they? What were the barriers to their social inclusion at project inception? What did the project do at its inception and during implementation to understand their situation? 2. Did the project improve the borrower's system and procedures for understanding the issues of excluded and vulnerable people or persons that benefited or were affected by the project?	1. What are the project targets related to the livelihood, voice, and social empowerment of excluded and vulnerable groups? 2. Did the project contribute to the livelihood, voice, and social empowerment of the excluded and vulnerable groups in project areas? If yes, what approaches worked and did not work? If no, what barred the project from doing so?	1. What project targets are for the ending of discriminatory (biased) norms, mindsets, policies, and structures impeding the three pillars of OP1? 2. Did the project contribute to ending these discriminatory norms, mindsets, policies, and structures? If yes, what approaches worked and did not work? If no, what barred the project from doing so?
OP2 (accelerating progress in gender equality) pillars: 1. Women's economic empowerment 2. Gender equality in human development 3. Gender equality in decision-making and leadership 4. Women's reduced time poverty and drudgery 5. Women's resilience to external shocks	3. Did the project aim to respond to gender inequality issues? If yes, who were the target beneficiaries? What did the project do at its inception and during implementation to understand their situation? What are their specific gender issues? 4. Did the project improve the borrower's system and procedures for understanding the issues of women that benefited or were affected by the project?	3. What are project targets related to women's livelihood, voice, and social empowerment? 4. Did the project contribute to women's livelihood, voice, and social empowerment? If yes, what approaches worked and did not work? If no, what barred the project from doing so? 5. What roles did women and men play in the empowerment of women?	3. What are project targets for ending discriminatory (gender-biased) norms, mindsets, policies, and structures impeding the five pillars of OP2? 4. Did the project contribute to ending these discriminatory gender norms, mindsets, policies, and structures? If yes, what approaches worked and did not work? If no, what barred the project from doing so?

continued on next page

Table continued

Pillars of Strategy 2030 Operational Priorities 1 and 2 and Intersectionality	Areas for Gender Equality and Social Inclusion Impact Evaluation		
	Understand for Action	Empower for Change	Include for Opportunity
Intersection of gender inequality and other forms of exclusion and vulnerability	5. Did the project aim to respond to issues that reflect the intersection of gender inequality with other forms of exclusion and vulnerability and the intersection of these other forms of exclusion and vulnerability? If yes, who were the target beneficiaries? What did the project do at its inception and implementation to understand their situation? What are their specific gender equality and social inclusion issues? 6. Did the project improve the borrower's system and procedures for understanding the issues of women and girls or excluded and vulnerable groups that benefited or were affected by the project?	6. What are project targets related to the livelihood, voice, and social empowerment of women and disadvantaged groups experiencing intersecting inequalities? 7. Did the project contribute to their livelihood, voice, and social empowerment? If yes, what approaches worked and did not work? If no, what barred the project from doing so?	5. What are the project targets for ending discriminatory (gender biased) norms, mindsets, policies, and structures faced by women and groups experiencing intersecting inequalities? 6. Did the project contribute to the ending of these discriminatory gender norms, mindsets, policies, and structures? If yes, what approaches worked and did not work? If no, what barred the project from doing so?

OP1 = operational priority 1, OP2 = operational priority 2.

Source: Asian Development Bank (South Asia Department).

Appendix 2: ADB's Corporate Results Framework Indicators
Relevant to Gender Equality and Social Inclusion

CRF Levels	CRF Results Framework Indicators
Level 1 Results Framework Indicators	1. Population living on less than $1.90 a day (%, number) 2. Growth rates of household expenditure or income per capita among the bottom 40% and the total population (percentage points difference) 3. Annual growth rate of real GDP per capita in 2010 constant US dollars 4. Unemployment rate (%): a. Female, b. Male 5. Deaths attributed to climate-related and geophysical hazards (number) 6. Prevalence of stunting among children under 5 years (%) 7. Worldwide Governance Indicators
Level 2 Results Framework Indicators	
Strategy 2030 Level 2A, OP1: Addressing remaining poverty and reducing inequalities	1. People benefiting from improved health services, education services or social protection (number) 2. Jobs generated 3. Poor and vulnerable people with improved standards of living (number)
Strategy 2030 OP2: Accelerating Progress in gender equality	**Level 2A (Strategy 2030 Operational Priority Results)** 1. Skilled jobs for women generated (number) 2. Women and girls completing secondary and tertiary education and/or other training (number) 3. Women represented in decision-making structures and processes (number) 4. Women and girls with increased time savings (number) 5. Women and girls with increased resilience to climate change, disasters and other external shocks (number) **Level 2B (ADB's Operational Management)** 6. Completed operations delivering intended gender equality results (%) (sovereign and nonsovereign)
Strategy 2030 Level 2A, OP3 to OP7	**OP3: Tackling climate change, building climate and disaster resilience, and enhancing environmental sustainability** 1. People with strengthened climate and disaster resilience (number) 2. People benefiting from strengthened environmental sustainability (number) **OP4: Making cities more livable** 3. People benefiting from improved services in urban areas (number) 4. Entities with improved urban planning and financial sustainability (number) 5. Zones with improved urban environment, climate resilience and disaster risk management (number) **OP5: Promoting rural development and food security** 6. People benefiting from increased rural investment (number) 7. Farmers with improved market access (number) **OP6: Strengthening governance and institutional capacity** 8. Entities with improved service delivery (number) **OP7: Fostering regional cooperation and integration** 9. Regional public goods initiatives successfully reducing cross-border environmental or health risks, or providing regional access to education services (number)

CRF= corporate results framework, GESI = gender equality and social inclusion, OP = operational priority

Source: ADB. 2019. *ADB Corporate Results Framework, 2019-2024: Policy Paper*. Manila.

Appendix 3: Guide for Preparing the Terms of Reference of the Gender Equality and Social Inclusion Impact Evaluation or Assessment

Key Section	Contents and Decision-Making Points	Guide/Reference
I. Introduction	1. Overview of the project, including the GESI issues the project sought to address and target beneficiaries, and its gender categorization 2. Rationale of the GESI impact evaluation or assessment: results of the project GESI evaluability assessment 3. Significance of the GESI impact evaluation 4. Type of GESI impact evaluation or assessment: whether nimble or long term 5. Who will do the evaluation or assessment? Will a consulting firm be engaged, or will in-house resources (project staff) be mobilized?	• Project documents • Sections I-III., paras. 4-16 • Box • Table 1
II. Purpose and nature of the evaluation or assessment	1. Purpose of the GESI impact evaluation or assessment: overall evaluation or assessment question(s) (including hypotheses for the quantitative method) 2. Nature: quantitative, qualitative, or mixed method 3. Participatory or not	Section IV, paras. 17–21
III. Evaluation or assessment design	1. If the quantitative method: randomized controlled trial or quasi-experimental design or other 2. If the qualitative method: phenomenology or narrative analysis or ethnography or other 3. If the mixed method: what are the quantitative and qualitative designs and what is the dominant method (quantitative or qualitative)	Section IV, paras. 22–27 Table 2
	Unit of analysis: individuals, households, or communities	Para. 28
IV. Overview of evaluation methods	Sampling method	Paras. 29–33
	Data sources and collection methods	Paras. 34–38, Table 3
	Data collation methods	Paras. 39–43, Table 4, and Table 5
	Data analysis methods	Paras. 44–49
V. Report outline	Report outline and points to cover in each section of the report	Table 6
VI. Dissemination Strategy	With whom will the findings be shared, and how	Para. 51
VII. Detailed tasks and qualifications of the impact evaluation team or consulting firm	1. Tasks will include the finalization of the GESI impact evaluation plan (parts II to VI) and, if participatory, will include the participation plan 2. Qualifications: years of experience in GESI impact evaluation using the quantitative, qualitative, or mixed method and in the participatory GESI impact evaluation process; proven publishing record; postgraduate degree in relevant field(s) for members of the team	

GESI = gender equality and social inclusion.

Note: The table provides the key points to consider when preparing the terms of reference for the GESI impact evaluation. The third column (Guide/Reference) refers to the parts of the guidance note that may be used as a guide.

Source: Asian Development Bank (South Asia Department).

www.ingramcontent.com/pod-product-compliance
Lightning Source LLC
Chambersburg PA
CBHW050057220326
41599CB00045B/7452